THE SCIENCE BEHIND BATMAN'S TOOLS

DC COMICS™
SUPER HEROES

by
Agnieszka Biskup

BATMAN created by
Bob Kane with Bill Finger

SCIENCE BEHIND BATMAN

Curious Fox
a capstone company-publishers for children

Published by Curious Fox, an imprint of Capstone Global Library Limited, 7 Pilgrim Street, London, EC4V 6LB –
Registered company number: 6695582

www.curious-fox.com

STAR37306

ISBN 978 1 78202 544 3
20 19 18 17 16
10 9 8 7 6 5 4 3 2 1

British Library Cataloguing in Publication Data
A full catalogue record for this book is available from the British Library.

Editorial Credits
Christopher Harbo, editor; Hilary Wacholz, designer; Wanda Winch, media researcher;
Tori Abraham, production specialist

Artwork by Luciano Vecchio and Ethen Beavers

Photo Credits
Alamy: louise murray, 20, National Geographic Creative/Gregory A. Harlin, 13 (top), WaterFrame, 21; Getty
Images: AFP/Kazhuiro Nogi, 9; Shutterstock: digitalreflections, 13 (bottom), farres, 8, Gavran333, 7, Joe White,
14 (t), PinkBlue, 17 (t), Sergio Schnitzler, 12, Tooykrub, 15; Thinkstock: manxman, 14 (b); U.S. Army photo by
Markus Rauchenberger, 11; U.S. Marine Corps photo by Cpl. David Hernandez, 18; U.S. Navy photo by John
Narewski, 19, Mass Communications Specialist Seaman Martin Carey, 16

Printed in China.

CONTENTS

INTRODUCTION

ULTIMATE TOOL KIT

Many super heroes use special tools to fight crime. Wonder Woman has her Golden Lasso of Truth. Green Lantern uses a power ring. But Batman carries a whole tool kit. His Utility Belt is packed with amazing gadgets. Best of all, much of it exists in the real world.

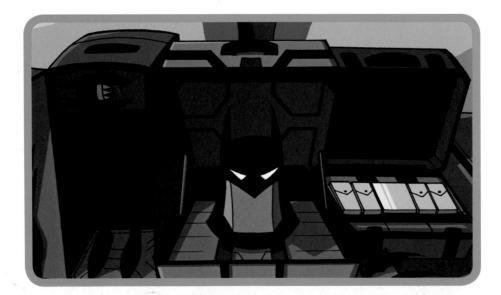

Green Lantern's power ring harnesses his willpower to do almost anything.

Batman's Utility Belt carries all of his tools, gadgets and weapons.

Wonder Woman's Golden Lasso of Truth forces anyone held by it to tell the truth.

CHAPTER 1
BATARANGS AND GRAPNELS

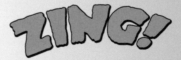

ZING!

Batman carries several
types of Batarang.

Some Batarangs return like **boomerangs**. A boomerang's wings tip sideways as it spins through the air. This **motion** causes it to curve in flight. Thrown correctly, a boomerang will return to the thrower.

A boomerang is held correctly when its curve points towards the thrower.

Some boomerangs have three or four wings. More wings allow boomerangs to turn in tighter circles.

boomerang curved stick that spins and turns in flight; some boomerangs are made to rcturn to the thrower

motion moving or being moved

The Dark Knight often uses Batarangs to smash windows and lights. Japanese **ninjas** once used shuriken in a similar way. These throwing weapons were usually thin, star-shaped metal plates. With a flick of the wrist, ninjas sent shuriken spinning through the air.

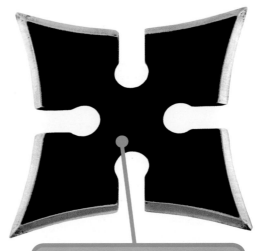

FACT

Some shuriken were straight, spike-like blades. They were thrown overarm, like a cricket ball.

Star-shaped shuriken had between three and eight razor-sharp points.

Modern-day ninja Jinichi Kawakami displays a collection of traditional Japanese weapons.

ninja someone who is highly trained in Japanese martial arts and stealth

Batman uses a **grapnel** gun to help him climb buildings. It **launches** a hook and rope onto a roof.

In our world, soldiers use grappling hooks too. The US Army even has a tool for launching them. The T-PLS can fire a grappling hook and rope 37 metres (120 feet) into the air.

A soldier practises throwing a grappling hook during training.

grapnel hook with four or five prongs
launch send something into the air

CHAPTER 2
BOLAS AND BOMBS

When villains run, the Caped Crusader uses bolas to trip them up. A bola has several weights connected by cords. People have hunted with bolas for thousands of years. These weapons helped catch animals by wrapping around their legs or wings.

Some traditional bolas used leather sacks filled with stones for weights.

Ancient hunters used bolas to catch prey.

FACT

A modern outdoor game is played by throwing two-ball bolas onto a plastic ladder.

Batman uses smoke bombs to cover his escapes. In our world, some fireworks are also smoke bombs. These hollow clay or cardboard containers are packed with smoke-making chemicals. When lit, the chemicals burn to release thick clouds of smoke.

Smoke bombs come in different sizes and shapes and can release many colours.

FACT

Soldiers often use smoke **grenades** as signals.
They can release red, orange, green, blue,
purple, black or white smoke.

grenade small bomb that can be thrown or launched

The Dark Knight also distracts enemies with flash grenades. Soldiers and police officers use flashbang grenades to cause confusion. Flashbangs release a blinding light and an ear-splitting bang. The blast can cause short-term blindness and hearing loss.

A soldier throws a flashbang during a training exercise.

Soldiers and police officers sometimes use flashbangs during hostage situations.

FACT

A flashbang's blast is louder than a jet engine. It can affect the **fluid** in the inner ear and cause people to lose their sense of balance.

fluid liquid or gas substance that flows

POP!

POP!

POP!

CHAPTER 3

PERISCOPES AND REBREATHERS

Batman's periscope helps him to see around walls in secret. Periscopes use mirrors to **reflect** light around corners. Light coming into the periscope bounces off one mirror and travels to a second mirror. This mirror shows the user what's happening around the corner.

A solider using a hand-held periscope.

photonics masts

reflect bounce off an object

For underwater missions, the Caped Crusader relies on his rebreather. These devices allow divers to rebreathe their own air. Rebreathers remove harmful gases that the diver breathes out. Leftover **oxygen** is then breathed in again.

A diver uses a rebreather to move through the water.

oxygen colourless gas in the air that people and animals need to live

A rebreather doesn't release bubbles the way scuba gear does.

From Batarangs to rebreathers, Batman's Utility Belt carries everything he needs. Many real-world tools are as amazing as those used by the Dark Knight himself.

GLOSSARY

boomerang curved stick that spins and turns in flight; some boomerangs are made to return to the thrower

fluid liquid or gas substance that flows

grapnel hook with four or five prongs

grenade small bomb that can be thrown or launched

launch send something into the air

motion moving or being moved

ninja someone who is highly trained in Japanese martial arts and stealth

oxygen colourless gas in the air that people and animals need to live

reflect bounce off an object

READ MORE

Avoid Being a Ninja Warrior! (Danger Zone), John Malam (Book House, 2012)

Drones, Henry Brook (Usborne, 2016)

Great Electronic Gadget Designs (Iconic Designs), Richard Spilsbury (Raintree, 2015)

How to Draw Batman and His Friends and Foes (Drawing DC Super Heroes), Aaron Sautter (Raintree, 2015)

Special Forces (Heroic Jobs), Ellen Labrecque (Raintree, 2013)

Spying, Henry Brook (Usborne, 2013)

INDEX

READ THEM ALL!

THE SCIENCE BEHIND BATMAN'S UNIFORM
by Agnieszka Biskup

THE SCIENCE BEHIND BATMAN'S GROUND VEHICLES
by Tammy Enz

THE SCIENCE BEHIND BATMAN'S FLYING MACHINES
by Tammy Enz

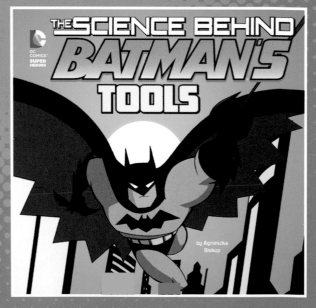

THE SCIENCE BEHIND BATMAN'S TOOLS
by Agnieszka Biskup